•• **Debra Powell**

Common
mistakes at

CAE

... and how to avoid them

CAMBRIDGE
UNIVERSITY PRESS

CAMBRIDGE UNIVERSITY PRESS
Cambridge, New York, Melbourne, Madrid, Cape Town, Singapore, São Paulo, Delhi

Cambridge University Press
The Edinburgh Building, Cambridge CB2 8RU, UK

www.cambridge.org
Information on this title: www.cambridge.org/9780521603775

First published 2005
6th printing 2009

Printed in Dubai by Oriental Press

A catalogue record for this publication is available from the British Library

ISBN 978-0-521-60377-5 paperback

Designed and produced by Kamae Design, Oxford

Contents

Perfect tenses: simple or continuous?

Tick the correct sentence in each pair.

1. a Global weather patterns have changed for many years.
   b Global weather patterns have been changing for many years.
2. a I'd stayed at a hotel for six months when I bought my house.
   b I'd been staying at a hotel for six months when I bought my house.

We use the simple aspect of tenses for actions which we think are:
- finished: *I've done my homework.* (the homework is finished)
- permanent: *I've lived in England for 10 years. I've worked for this company for most of that time.* (I think I will remain in England and continue to work for the same company)

We use the continuous aspect of tenses for actions which we think are:
- unfinished or in progress: *I've been doing my homework. (it isn't finished yet)*
- temporary: *I've been living in England for six months. I've been working as an au pair.* (I think I will leave England one day – my job is temporary)

We use past perfect tenses to connect two past actions, and past perfect continuous when one event interrupts another:
I'd been waiting for twenty minutes when the bus arrived.
☆ The simple or continuous aspect applies across the entire tense system.

2 Correct the mistake below.

I've written this essay all day.

I've .... all day.

Complete the sentences with the correct form of the verb in brackets.

1. I .... *(live)* here all my life and never want to leave.
2. I .... *(attend)* a beginner's class in Spanish for six weeks.
3. We .... *(drive)* for hours when we spotted the hotel.
4. I .... *(take)* the train for a long time. I prefer to drive.
5. Mr Georgiou .... *(work)* for the company for twenty years when he retired.
6. The city I grew up in .... *(changed)* so much, I hardly recognise it any more.
7. I .... *(work)* in an office for the past month, but my profession is acting.
8. She .... *(always / take)* good care of her finances.

5

2 Perfect tenses: active or passive?

1 Tick the correct sentence in each pair.

1 a Eating habits have changed dramatically in the last decade.
   b Eating habits have been changed dramatically in the last decade.
2 a Smoking has shown to be a cause of cancer.
   b Smoking has been shown to be a cause of cancer.

We use active forms of perfect tenses (*had / has* + past participle) to describe a situation which has changed:
*It's really stormy – the roof **has blown** off!*

We use passive forms of perfect tenses (*has / had been* + past participle) to describe something which happened in the past and has a clear effect on the present:
*The effect of diet on health **has been proved**.*

We use active forms of perfect tenses to describe a situation which has changed by itself. We use passive forms when the situation has been changed by someone or something in particular. Compare:
*Attitudes to religion **have changed**.*
*His attitude to life **has been changed** by the accident.*

We use the present perfect for activities which have a clear effect on the present. For finished activities with no connection to the present, use the past simple. Compare:
*Last week's football match **was cancelled**.* (we are thinking of the past)
*Today's football match **has been cancelled**.* (we are thinking of the present – there is n[o] match today)

2 Correct the mistake below.

I'm afraid your flight _has been_ delayed.

3 Underline the most suitable tense.

1 The economic situation *has improved / has been improved* considerably. ∨
2 The light bulb *was invented / had been invented* by Thomas Edison.
3 I *had applied / applied* for the job last week and now I have been invited for interview.
4 The house in which he lived *had left / had been left* to him by his mother.
5 Since losing his job his lifestyle *has changed / has been changed* considerably.
6 It *has proved / has been* proved that caffeine affects heart rate and blood pressure.
7 We *have organised / have been organised* a leaving party for Alex. ∨
8 He *had handed in / handed in / has handed in* his notice last week.

6

Give or have?

1 Tick the correct sentence in each pair.

1 a Madonna gave an excellent performance. —
  b Madonna had an excellent performance.

2 a Television can give a great effect on the family.
  b Television can have a great effect on the family. —

We use *give* to form collocations with certain nouns with an active meaning, i.e. 'to deliver':

- *give a performance / speech / talk*: The band **gave a great performance**.
- *give information / advice / an example / an explanation*:
  He **gave no explanation** for his poor performance.

In more formal speech or writing, we often replace *give* with other verbs:

- *give / deliver a speech; give / express an opinion; give / hold a lecture*:
  The lecture **will be held** in Room 336.

We use *have* with certain nouns to form collocations with the sense of ownership:

- *have a(n) problem / chance / opportunity / experience / career / baby*:
  If I **have a chance**, I'll travel.
- *have an idea / impression / opinion*: Do you **have an opinion** on hunting?
- *have an advantage / effect / impact*:
  You **have the advantage**, I'm afraid. My comments **had no effect** on him.
- *have a meal / break / appointment / trip*: I like to **have a light breakfast**.

We use *have*, not *spend*, in certain phrases to do with time:

- *have a great time / a pleasant evening*: She **had a great time** in Ibiza.

2 Correct the mistake below.

Come on over. We're giving a barbecue.

Come on over. We're ....

3 Correct the sentences with a form of *give* or *have* as appropriate.

1 Have you taken breakfast yet? ....
2 We spent a great time at the party. ....
3 Maria holds a great party, don't you think? ....
4 The lectures were made by a series of experts. ....
5 The book has made a great impact on public opinion. ....
6 I'm tired. Are we making a break? ....
7 Not everyone can make a good career. ....
8 If you don't understand, I'll show you another example. ....

TEST 1

1 Complete each sentence with a form of *give* or *have* and one of the words in the box. Use each word only once.

advice	appointment	experience	explanation
idea	problems	speech	

1 Traditionally, the best man .... a(n) .... at the wedding reception.

2 A: Where are you going?
   B: I .... a(n) .... with the bank manager.

3 A: How was your holiday?
   B: Not great. We .... a lot of .... (s) with the hotel.

4 The manager couldn't .... us any .... for the lack of facilities advertised in the brochure.

5 It's important for you to .... a(n) .... of how the firm is organised before you start working here.

6 Having .... no .... of raising children, I wouldn't like to .... you .... on how to deal with your son's problem.

2 Complete the dialogue. Put the verbs in brackets in either the present perfect simple or present perfect continuous tense.

Mark: Anna, I haven't seen you since College! What (1) .... *(do)*?

Anna: Mark! What a surprise! (2) .... *(work)* in France. And you?

Mark: Well, (3) .... *(have)* a few jobs abroad, but I'm in London now and (4) .... *(teach)* at a school in Hampstead for the past few months.

Anna: That's great! Do you think you'll stay there?

Mark: Hard to say. (5) .... *(always / want)* to live in the Far East, and lately (6) .... *(think)* about applying for work in Hong Kong.

Anna: (7) .... *(hear)* it's a great place to live. Listen, there's a new play showing at the Art Centre. (8) .... *(see)* it?

Mark: Not yet. (9) .... *(not / be)* out much since I started this new job. Hey, you and Sarah were good mates. (10) .... *(ring)* her yet? Maybe the three of us could go together.

Anna: Good idea. Give me your number …

8

3 Read Mark's email to a colleague, Alex. Use the information in it to complete the minutes. Use an appropriate passive verb for each gap.

Hi Alex

Sorry you weren't able to make the staff meeting. Some good news! We got our exam results this week and they were much better than last year's – 10% more of our students got a pass. By the way, there've been a lot of complaints from students about other students arriving late, so we've decided that teachers should send late arrivals to the library. What do you think? Finally, you know the party that we'd scheduled for 15 Oct – we've postponed it to the 22nd.

See you soon.

Mark

Minutes

1 The Cambridge examination results, which (1) .... this week, show a pass result (2) .... by 10% more students this year than last.

2 Complaints (3) .... by a number of students that their classes are being disturbed by other students who arrive late. It (4) .... that students who arrive more than 10 minutes late should be sent to the library to work.

3 The date for the mid-term party, which (5) .... for 15 October, (6) .... to 22 October.

4 In each line of the text put the verb in brackets in an appropriate perfect tense.

THE NEWS TODAY

Fresh outbreaks of violence *(report)* today in the country of Mornavia, where rebel forces *(surround)* the capital city. Continued fighting *(take)* place throughout the day and night. The President *(announce)* that his government may step down in response to the popular support which *(give)* to the rebel forces, though previously he *(deny)* any possibility of surrender. Tensions in the country *(build)*, but violence erupted during the elections last year. To date, the cost of the conflict *(be)* high. Countless lives *(be)* lost in the fighting and industry in the country *(virtually / come)* to a halt.

1 ....
2 ....
3 ....
4 ....
5 ....
6 ....
7 ....
8 ....
9 ....
10 ....

5 Are these sentences right or wrong? Correct those which are wrong.

1 This year's trade figures had been announced yesterday. ....

2 We spent a wonderful time at the beach yesterday. ....

3 Look at the weather! It's rained all day! ....

4 I complained about the service and they agreed to have my money back. ....

5 Going to war had an impact on the government's popularity. ....

6 David Buckingham has announced his retirement from professional sport. ....

7 The announcement has been made a short time ago. ....

4 How many objects does the verb need?

1 Tick the correct sentence in each pair.

1 a I'm writing to give information and advice.
  b I'm writing to give you information and advice.
2 a I regret to inform that there have been complaints about the service.
  b I regret to inform you that there have been complaints about the service.

Transitive verbs require an object. Some verbs need two objects to complete their meaning, an indirect object, which generally comes first, and a direct object:

* *send / give (someone something):*
  *I **gave him the money** I owed. / **I've sent you an email**.*
  ☆ We can often put the direct object (the thing) first, followed by a preposition:
  *I **gave the money to him**. / I **sent an email to her**.* (not ~~I gave to him the money / I sent to her an email~~)

Other verbs taking two objects are:

* *assure (someone) that + clause / assure (someone) of (something):*
  *I **assure you that** we'll do everything we can to help. / I **assure you of** our best intentions.*
* *inform (someone) that + clause / inform (someone) of / about (something):*
  *This letter is to **inform you that** I am not satisfied / **inform you of** my dissatisfaction.*
* *tell (someone) (something) / tell (someone) that + clause / tell (someone) how / why,* etc.:
  *He **told me a lie**. / He **told me that** he wasn't married. / He **told me where** he lived.*

2 Correct the mistake below.

I'd like to tell about my experiences working for a large multinational.

I'd like ....

3 Are the sentences right or wrong? Correct those which are wrong.

1 I give to you my word that your secret is safe. ....
2 The firm assured Nadia of their complete trust in her ability. ....
3 I sent to her a message last week. ....
4 Let me give some advice. ....
5 Thank you for telling about your stay in Japan. ....
6 James told to the police the truth. ....
7 He told where he spent Friday night. ....
8 The police informed him that he wasn't a suspect. ....

Do I use the gerund or infinitive with the verb + object?

1 **Tick the correct sentence in each pair.**

1 a Let them know when you're arriving.
  b Let them to know when you're arriving.
2 a I can't stop you to leave if you want to go.
  b I can't stop you leaving if you want to go.

Some verbs need an object followed by an infinitive with *to*:
- *allow / authorise (someone) to do (something)*:
  The ticket **authorises / allows you to travel** for one month.
- *get / force / help (someone) to do (something)*:
  I **got the doctor to make** a house call.   Poor health **forced him to give up** smoking.
- *ask / tell (someone) to do (something)*: Can I **ask you to do something** for me?

Some verbs take an infinitive without *to*:
- *let / make (someone) do (something)*:
  We can't **let you leave**.   You can't **make me go**.

Other verbs need an object followed by a gerund:
- *stop / prevent someone (from) doing something* in the future:
  The police put up barriers to **prevent people entering** the house.
- *see / hear / watch / feel (someone) doing (something)*:
  I **watched the children playing** in the park.

2 Correct the mistake below.

I'm afraid ....

3 **Underline the correct form.**

1 How can we get them *change / to change / changing* their minds?
2 Children are not allowed *travel / to travel / travelling* unaccompanied.
3 There's nothing preventing you *take / to take / taking* a holiday.
4 I won't let you *make / to make / making* such a stupid mistake.
5 I'm asking you *consider / to consider / considering* the consequences.
6 It's impossible to make someone *do / to do / doing* something they don't want to do.
7 I can hear music *play / to play / playing* in the background.
8 I wish I could stop her from *feel / to feel / feeling* sorry for herself!

11

6 Give, provide or offer?

1 Tick the correct sentence in each pair.

1. a We wish to complain about the service given by your company.
   b We wish to complain about the service provided by your company.
2. a The service you provided did not match your promises.
   b The service you offered did not match your promises.

We use *provide*:

- as a general rule, to talk about services which have already happened:
  *The information you requested **is provided** in the brochure we sent you.*
- instead of *give* in more formal contexts:
  *They have promised to **provide** us with a friendly service.* (not ~~to give us a friendly service~~)

We use *offer*:

- to talk about possible services which someone might choose in the future:
  *We can **offer** (you) an excellent discount (if you choose our service).*

We use *offer* and *provide* with two objects:

- *offer (someone something) / offer (something) to (someone)*:
  *They **offer people** with financial problems **free legal advice**.*
  *They **offer free legal advice to people** with financial problems.*
- *provide (someone) with (something) / provide (something) for (someone)*:
  *The hotel does not **provide guests with an evening meal**.*
  *The hotel does not **provide an evening meal** (for its guests).*

2 Correct the mistake below.

Of course there's a place for your son. In fact, we can give individual tuition.

SCHOOL OF LANGUAGES

In fact, we can ....

3 Complete the sentences below with the correct form of *give*, *offer* or *provide*.

1. We can .... the food if you can supply the entertainment.
2. If you sign the contract today, we can .... a 10% discount.
3. Morning and evening meals are .... as part of the service.
4. We're .... you a better deal than you'll find anywhere else.
5. It's our policy to .... clients with the best service possible.
6. For a small surcharge, we .... clients the option of bringing a guest.
7. I've .... you all the information I have available.
8. Would you .... me the name of your manager, please.

TEST 2

1 Underline the most appropriate word.

1 The hotel *gives / provides / offers* evening entertainment for its guests.

2 The company promises to *give / provide / offer* meals made from fresh ingredients.

3 Have they *given / provided / offered* you a discount if you sign today?

4 Would you *give / provide / offer* me your telephone number?

5 Catering services aim to *give / provide / offer* good food at low cost.

6 They're *offering / providing* cash prizes to winners of the best competition.

7 There's no point in further negotiation. These are the best terms I can *give / provide / offer*.

8 We are *offering / providing* you the chance to buy the complete set at half price.

2 Complete Suzanne's email by filling in the gaps with an appropriate word where necessary.

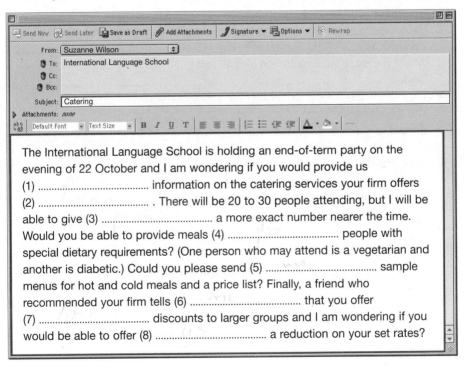

The International Language School is holding an end-of-term party on the evening of 22 October and I am wondering if you would provide us
(1) .... information on the catering services your firm offers
(2) .... There will be 20 to 30 people attending, but I will be able to give (3) .... a more exact number nearer the time. Would you be able to provide meals (4) .... people with special dietary requirements? (One person who may attend is a vegetarian and another is diabetic.) Could you please send (5) .... sample menus for hot and cold meals and a price list? Finally, a friend who recommended your firm tells (6) .... that you offer (7) .... discounts to larger groups and I am wondering if you would be able to offer (8) .... a reduction on your set rates?

3 Is each line in the letter below right or wrong? Correct those which are wrong. Sometimes there is a word missing, a wrong word or a word which is not needed.

> Thank you for your letter inquiring about our catering service.
> Not only can we provide you a full range of services, we can
> offer to you a 10% discount on numbers over 20 if you
> send to us confirmation of your booking within 30 days. We can
> also provide dishes to meet special dietary requirements if you
> inform in advance. I enclose a full price list. We will be happy
> to provide with further information on request. In closing, I'd
> like to assure to you of our best intentions.

1 ....
2 ....
3 ....
4 ....
5 ....
6 ....
7 ....
8 ....

4 Rewrite the second sentence, using a form of the word in brackets, so that it means the same as the first.

1 His doctor made him go on a strict diet. *(force)*
   His doctor ....

2 His company gave him permission to take unpaid leave from work. *(authorise)*
   His company ....

3 Would you do something for me please? *(ask)*
   Could I .... ?

4 The school decided not to let him take the exam. *(allow)*
   The school decided ....

5 The police didn't allow witnesses to leave the scene of the crime. *(prevent)*
   The police ....

6 They forced me to sign the document. *(make)*
   They ....

7 No matter what I do, my computer won't work. *(get)*
   I can't ....

8 They promised to help me in any way they could. *(assure)*
   They ....

5 Are the sentences right or wrong? Correct those which are wrong.

1 I could hear music playing in the background. ....

2 My parents refused to allow me going out on a school night. ....

3 I could smell food cook when I walked through the door. ....

4 They don't allow their children staying up past nine o'clock. ....

5 You haven't told why you've come to see me. ....

6 I'd like to inform you that I've decided not to attend the course. ....

7 The tour bus stopped for an hour to allow passengers going to the shops.
   ....

8 His health prevents him to work full time. ....

14

How do I use *must* and *have to*?

1 Tick the correct sentence in each pair.

1 a You mustn't take lessons to learn to cook.

   b You don't have to take lessons to learn to cook.

2 a I must have wear a suit and tie in my last job.

   b I had to wear a suit and tie in my last job.

All modal verbs used to express certainty in the past take *have* + past participle:
*You **must be** Ellen's sister – you look just like her.* (present)
*You **must have had** a good time last night – you look terrible!* (past)

The negative form of this use of *must* is *can't do* or *can't have done*:
*You **can't be** certain she's guilty – what proof do you have?* (present)
*The party **can't have been** any good – they were home early.* (past)

When *must* is used to express obligation, the past form is *had to* + infinitive:
*You **must see** a doctor – you're obviously not well.* (present)
*I **had to leave** work early yesterday – I was ill.* (past)

The negative forms of this use of *must* are:
* *mustn't do*, for negative obligation, and *don't have to do*, for absence of obligation:
  *You **mustn't play** with matches – it's dangerous!* (present)
  *You **don't have to go** to school today – it's a holiday.* (present)
* *didn't have to do* for absence of obligation:
  *I **didn't have to wear** a suit last night – it was an informal dinner.* (past)

2 Correct the mistake below.

Jamie's in bed, Doctor, and he must have stayed at home yesterday, as well.

Jamie's in bed, Doctor, and ....

3 Complete the sentences. Use a form of *must, have to* or *can't*. It may be necessary to change the form of the word in brackets.

1 That was an awful accident – you .... *(be)* very frightened.

2 We .... *(argue)* anymore – it's affecting the children.

3 The fridge is empty – they .... *(eat)* all the food!

4 I .... *(go)* out last night, though I'd rather have stayed at home.

5 You .... *(be)* serious! I don't believe you're saying that!

6 The wedding's tomorrow – you .... *(be)* feeling nervous.

7 You .... *(buy)* me a present, but how kind!

8 She .... *(tell)* him the truth or they wouldn't still be together.

15

8 Do I put the adverb before or after a modal verb?

1 Tick the correct sentence in each pair.

1 a I'm so tired, I can hardly keep my eyes open.
  b I'm so tired, I hardly can keep my eyes open.

2 a They won't probably arrive on time – they never do.
  b They probably won't arrive on time – they never do.

We usually put these adverbs immediately after the modal auxiliary verb:
- adverbs of time and frequency, e.g. *ever, sometimes, never, still, already, soon*:
  *You **will never learn** to speak English if you don't practise.*
  *I **can still see** the mess you left in the kitchen.*
- focusing adverbs, e.g. *also, only, even, just*:
  *I **can just reach** it if I stretch.*
- adverbs of degree, e.g. *barely, hardly*:
  *We **could barely manage** it in the time we had.*
  *We **could hardly have managed** it in less time.*
- adverbs of certainty, e.g. *definitely, probably, possibly*:
  *I **will probably see** you tonight.*
  These adverbs come before a contracted negative modal:
  *I **probably won't see** you at the party. / I **definitely can't meet** you.*

Adverbs of manner ending in *-ly*, e.g. *angrily, easily, happily*, can go after the modal verb or after all auxiliary verbs in a phrase:
*You **could have easily phoned** and told me where you were.*
*You **could easily have phoned** and told me where you were.*

2 Correct the mistake below.

Let's start again. You never will improve if you don't practise.

You ....

3 Add the adverb in brackets to the sentence.

1 You can live well with very little money. *(still)* ....
2 If you'd tried a little harder, you might have come first. *(even)* ....
3 I'd have agreed to help if you'd asked me. *(happily)* ....
4 It's tiny. You can see it close up. *(only)* ....
5 Travelling is fun, but it can be very expensive. *(also)* ....
6 I can't go out tonight. I've too much work. *(definitely)* ....
7 How could you go ahead with the party after what's happened? *(possibly)*
   ....
8 You shouldn't drink and drive. *(ever)* ....

How do I use *be supposed to*, *be expected to* and *be meant to*?

1. Tick the correct sentence in each pair.

1   a   You expected to dress smartly for a wedding.

    b   You are expected to dress smartly for a wedding.

2   a   Cars meant to make our lives easier.

    b   Cars are meant to make our lives easier.

Suppose is similar in meaning to 'think':
*I **suppose** we should be leaving. It's getting late.*

We use *expect to* to say we want or hope to do something, and *mean to* to say we intend to do something:
*We **expected to arrive** before 9.00, but we were late.*
*I **meant to meet** you as we agreed, but I was delayed.*

We use *be supposed to*, *be expected to* and *be meant to* to describe something someone else thinks we should / shouldn't do:
*You**'re not supposed to park** here.*
*You**'re expected to arrive** by 9.00 for the interview.*

When talking about the past we use *was / were supposed to / expected to / meant to* in place of *should have done* to criticise someone's behaviour:
*You're late! You **were supposed to be** here an hour ago.*
*You **were expected to wear** a suit for the meeting.*

We use *was / were supposed to* to say that events didn't happen the way we expected:
*We **were supposed to stop** somewhere nice for lunch.* (but we didn't)

2 Correct the mistake below.

The plane is suppose to be here an hour ago.

The plane ....

3 Underline the correct words.

1   Visitors *suppose / are supposed to* see the famous London sights.

2   Lunch *should / was supposed to* be in a typical English restaurant, but it wasn't.

3   I *was meant / meant* to send you a card for your birthday, but I forgot.

4   According to the invitation, what time *do we expect / are we expected* to arrive?

5   A famous actor *meant / was meant* to open this restaurant.

6   You're not *suppose to / supposed to* walk on the grass.

7   The result wasn't what it *was expected / expected* to be.

8   We *supposed / were supposed* to have a meeting.

TEST 3

1 Where necessary, add *am*, *is* or *are* to the sentence.

1 All meals meant to be inclusive in the price. ....

2 I expected to be home earlier, but the traffic was terrible. ....

3 I meant to bring my wallet, but I forgot. ....

4 Black cats supposed to be unlucky. ....

5 I suppose you think I'm mad, but I really want to leave my job. ....

6 Technology meant to make our lives easier. ....

7 You expected to dress smartly for the dinner tonight. ....

8 You supposed to exercise three times a week. ....

2 Complete the second sentence so it means the same as the first, using the words in brackets. Use between three and six words.

1 Doctors recommend a balanced diet. *(suppose)*
You .... eat a balanced diet

2 It's illegal to walk on the grass. *(suppose)*
You .... on the grass.

3 My parents thought I would become a doctor, but I didn't. *(expect)*
My parents .... , but I didn't

4 Why are they here? They weren't invited. *(mean)*
They .... here

5 People say that the number thirteen brings bad luck. *(suppose)*
The number .... unlucky

6 I always intended to go back to school and finish my education. *(mean)*
I always .... and finish my education.

7 According to the itinerary, we should have visited the castle yesterday. *(suppose)*
We .... the castle yesterday

8 They anticipate a lot of people will take part in the event. *(expect)*
A lot of .... in the event.

3 Underline the correct form.

1 You *can't / mustn't* be certain they're coming to the party.

2 You *mustn't / don't have to* lie to the tax office about your income – you could go to prison.

3 I *must have gone / had to go* out – I had an important meeting.

4 You *mustn't have / can't have* met my mother – she lives in Canada.

5 You *mustn't / don't have to* go to work on a public holiday.

6 You *can't be / can't have been* serious – surely you didn't mean what you said last night.

7 You *must be / must have been* tired when you arrived at the party.

8 They *must have gone out / had to go out* – their car's gone and the lights are out.

Reorder the words in brackets to complete Alan's letter to a friend.

Dear Alex

Just to let you know we're back from Barcelona. What a disappointment that was!

First of all, because the air conditioning in the hotel was broken, we had to leave our windows open. The hotel was very near the centre and the room was so noisy we (1) .... (sleep / hardly / could). Not that we wanted to look out of the window either – when we did we (2) .... (only / could / see) building sites!

I have to say that the itinerary wasn't bad, except that on our last afternoon it poured with rain. I know Sun Travel (3) .... (could / anticipated / hardly / have) bad weather, but they (4) .... (easily / had / have / could) a contingency plan. We (5) .... (had / should / have / also) more time at the Picasso Museum, as there was so much to see there. Oh, and the bus they provided was so cramped I (6) .... (move / could / barely) my legs, but by then I was tired of complaining.

Of course, I've asked for compensation, but the fact is nothing (7) .... (up / make / can / ever) for the disappointment of a ruined holiday. Truth is, we (8) .... (should / booked / never / have) a package holiday in the first place – Barcelona is such an easy place to get around next time we'll just get on a plane and find our own way round.

Hope you're well,

Best wishes

Alan

Are the sentences right or wrong? Correct those which are wrong.

1 She can't have left yet – her coat's still there. ....

2 She must have already arrived. ....

3 I won't see you at the meeting tonight probably. ....

4 She will admit never she was wrong. ....

5 She probably will win the competition. ....

6 We hardly could see the performance because we were sitting in the back row.
   ....

7 We can provide samples also of the menus for you to study. ....

8 I would have happily helped you if you'd asked me. ....

10 This or these?

1 Tick the correct sentence in each pair.

1 a People do too little exercise this days.

  b People do too little exercise these days.

2 a After all this advice, I hope you'll come to the right decision.

  b After all these advices, I hope you'll come to the right decision.

We use *these* in front of plural nouns, e.g. *children, mice, people, police*:
*Where did all **these people** come from?*

We use *this* in front of:

- singular countable nouns:
  *Why choose **this place** and time?*
- uncountable nouns:
  *I hope **this information** will be helpful.*

An uncountable noun has no plural form. Common uncountable nouns are: *chaos, evidence, ice, information, knowledge, lightning, literature, money, permission, pressure, success, thunder, traffic, work*

We use *this* and *these* with nouns that we think are close in space or time, and *that* and *those* with nouns that we see as more distant:
*Can you help me? There's a problem with **this software**.*
*I wish you'd stop playing with **that computer**!*

2 Correct the mistake below.

Look at all these traffic.

Look ....

3 Are the sentences right or wrong? Where necessary correct the underlined expressions

1 For all <u>these reasons</u>, I hope you will consider my proposal. ....

2 Don't you think <u>these money</u> should go in the bank? ....

3 In <u>this changing times</u>, we have to be prepared to adapt to new circumstances.
....

4 Can someone tell me why <u>this children</u> aren't in school? ....

5 We couldn't have achieved <u>this success</u> without your efforts. ....

6 People are doing very little exercise <u>this days</u>. ....

7 We hope to continue <u>these work</u> for many years. ....

8 How did you come by <u>these knowledges</u>? ....

How do I use *amount of, number of, kinds of,* etc.?

1 Tick the correct sentence in each pair.

1 a The amount of people suffering from this disease is increasing.

  b The number of people suffering from this disease is increasing.

2 a There are hundreds of different sort of butterflies.

  b There are hundreds of different sorts of butterflies.

We use *number of* before a plural countable noun:
*There are **a number of problems** to address.*

We use *amount of* or *quantity of* before an uncountable noun:
*We have a limited **amount of office equipment** to sell.*

We use plural forms like *kinds of, sorts of, types of*:
- after plural expressions like *all, different, many, these* and *various*:
  *I've taken **all kinds of courses**, but this was the best.*
- before plural nouns:
  *These **sorts of opportunities** don't come that often.*

We use the singular form *kind of, sort of, type of*:
- when we are talking about one sort, type or kind of thing:
  *There is a demand for **this kind of job**.*
- before uncountable nouns:
  ***This sort of information** can be dangerous in the wrong hands.*

2 Correct the mistake below.

I enjoy many different kind of music. And you?

I enjoy ....

3 Underline the correct words.

1 Don't forget to take a small *amount / number* of coins with you.

2 It's not safe to carry a large *amount / number* of cash with you.

3 This *kind / kinds* of high-paying job is difficult to find.

4 There were all *sort / sorts* of articles and books for sale.

5 A large *amount / number* of students took part in the demonstration.

6 There are plans to increase the *amount / number* of low-cost accommodation
available.

7 Our club needs more of this *type / types* of event.

8 Thanks, but I don't need that *sort / sorts* of advice.

12 Which article do I use?

1 Tick the correct sentence in each pair.

1. a The room they booked was at five-star hotel.
   b The room they booked was at a five-star hotel.
2. a The room was on a fourth floor and there was no lift.
   b The room was on the fourth floor and there was no lift.

We use *the*:
- when the identity of the person or thing is known to both the speaker and listener:
  The college canteen *serves reasonably priced food.*
- there can be only one of the person or thing referred to:
  We're studying Japan in ***the sixth century***.
- in front of superlative adjectives:
  Giving money isn't always ***the best way*** *to help people.*
- with countable or uncountable nouns:
  The report explains ***the current situation***. *It provided us with* ***the correct information.***

We use *a / an*:
- in front of singular countable nouns:
  We're looking for someone with ***an outgoing personality.***
  ☆ In front of uncountable nouns, we use *some*:
  He gave me ***some good advice***. (not ~~a good advice~~)
- with expressions like *a bit / few / little, a great time, a high standard, a certain way*:
  When she looks at me in ***a certain way***, *I know she's upset.*

2 Correct the mistake below.

I think I see some seats in a back row.

I think ....

3 Insert an appropriate article in each sentence.

1. Take the lift. Our apartment is on fourth floor. ....
2. We have automatic washing machine at home. ....
3. Our company has achieved best results ever this year. ....
4. I'll give you exact date when I know what it is. ....
5. Only bride's close friends were invited. ....
6. Confirm arrival time and gate before you leave home . ...
7. I called this meeting because I have few suggestions to make. ....
8. We've come to expect high standard of service. ....

1 Underline the correct words.

1 I hope you can follow *this / these* instructions.
2 Without your work, we couldn't achieve *this / these* success.
3 Would you put *this / that* cat down? It's filthy.
4 We all want to solve *this / these* problems.
5 Charities are designed to help *these / those* people that are suffering.
6 We'll continue *this / these* work until it's finished.
7 Look at that! Have you seen *these / those* stains on the carpet?
8 Who left *this / these* stuff here?

2 Are the sentences right or wrong? Correct those which are wrong.

1 A large amount of people in the world still suffer from hunger. ....
2 Our firm arranges different type of sporting events. ....
3 We have a large number of office equipments for sale. ....
4 What sort of jobs have you done? ....
5 I've done many different types of work. ....
6 Perhaps you should consider other kind of accommodation? ....
7 What kinds of information are you looking for? ....
8 He spends a large amount of money on entertainment. ....

3 Is each line in the extract below right or wrong? Correct those which are wrong. Sometimes there is a word missing, a wrong word, or a word which is not needed.

Last week I went shopping for the electronic gadgets and it's   1 ....
amazing what you can spend your money on this days. There   2 ....
were all kind of electronic equipment for sale, everything from   3 ....
an electronic cube which will forecast the weather to a solar   4 ....
powered briefcase which will charge electronic equipment inside   5 ....
the case. However, a gadget I liked the best was the walking desk,   6 ....
which has the treadmill and exercise bike installed underneath.   7 ....
They say an office worker like me could walk four to five miles   8 ....
in an average work day. Imagine that!

4 Complete the extract by writing *a*, *an* or *the* in the space provided. Sometimes no word is needed.

What's (1) .... weather doing? We don't have to watch
(2) .... weather report to find out – all we need to do is
look at our weather cubes. Currently (3) .... most popular
gadget in Japan, (4) .... battery-powered device is
(5) .... four-inch cube which can predict (6) ....
weather up to eight hours in advance. (7) .... cube gives
(8) .... 12- to 24- hour forecast via easy-to-read symbols
– clouds, rain, sun – displayed on (9) .... LCD screen.
(10) .... device can predict (11) .... rain, features
(12) .... snow possibility alarm, and will even display
sunrise and sunset times in cities around (13) .... world.
Would you go on (14) .... picnic without one?
(15) .... weather cube is (16) .... essential
travel accessory.

You, your, yours, or you're?

1 Tick the correct sentence in each pair.

1 a I'm sure your going to be pleased.
   b I'm sure you're going to be pleased.
2 a Our monthly repayment plan can save you money.
   b Our monthly repayment plan can save you're money.

We use *you* in place of a noun. *You* refers to the person or people being addressed:
*I wish **you** all the best.*

We use *your* in front of a noun:
*I've read **your brochure**.*

We use *yours*:
- instead of *your* + noun to show that something belongs to the person or people being addressed:
  *This coat is mine and that one is **yours**.*
- at the end of letters:
  Yours** faithfully / **Yours** sincerely / **Yours

You're is a contracted form and means 'you are':
***You're** always the last to leave a party!*

2 Correct the mistake below.

Thank you for you're attention.

abcdefghijk

123456

Thank ....

3 Complete the sentences with *you, you're, your* or *yours*.

1 Formal letters are signed ' .... faithfully'.
2 It doesn't belong to me. It's ....
3 Thank .... for .... letter.
4 The information in .... article was wrong.
5 In .... advertisement, ... promised many things.
6 I hope .... going to finish that before you leave.
7 Having read .... comments, I agree with ....
8 I'm writing to .... to complain.

25

14 Opportunity, possibility or chance?

1 Tick the correct sentence in each pair.

1 a The job gave me the possibility to travel to Scotland.
   b The job gave me the opportunity to travel to Scotland.
2 a When you have the opportunity, ask your father for his advice.
   b When you have the occasion, ask your father for his advice.

We use *opportunity* for a situation in which it's possible to do something you want to do:
*I have **the opportunity to study** abroad / **of going** to College.*
Collocations are *the earliest (first) opportunity, equal opportunity, a unique opportunity.*
☆ An *occasion* is a particular time when something happens:
*A birthday is a special **occasion**.*

We use *a possibility* for something that might or might not happen:
*There's **a possibility of rain** tonight / **that it will rain** tonight.*

The meaning of *chance* can overlap with the meanings of *possibility* and *opportunity*,
but *chance* may be used less formally:
*I know we're late, but is there any **chance (possibility) of catching** the train?*
*This is your **chance (opportunity) to do** what you've always wanted.*

Collocations are a *slim / slight / faint chance*, a *second chance*:
*I know I disappointed you, but please give me **a second chance**.*
☆ We use *have a chance* but not ~~have a possibility~~, and *grab* or *seize an opportunity*,
but not ~~grab a chance~~.

2 Correct the mistake below.

Thanks for giving me a second opportunity. I won't disappoint you.

HM PRISON

Thanks ....

3 Underline the correct words.

1 We want to improve our *chances / opportunities* of winning future contracts.
2 Everyone here has the *chance / possibility* to learn a second language.
3 Everyone should have equal *opportunities / possibilities* in education.
4 There was no *opportunity / possibility* for him to be entered for the exam.
5 There is a(n) *opportunity / possibility* it will snow tonight.
6 Thank you for this *occasion / opportunity* to broaden my knowledge.
7 Nursing gives one the *chance / possibility* to help others.
8 Going to a party is a great *occasion / opportunity* to meet new people.

Commonly confused nouns

1 Tick the correct sentence in each pair.

1 a ◯ We'd like to invite you to our next event, which will be held in May.
   b We'd like to invite you to our next activity, which will be held in May.

2 a ◯ Keeping fit is an important activity in the local area.
   b Keeping fit is an important event in the local area.

Activity or *event*?
An *activity* is something organised for people to take part in, e.g. a sport:
*The centre offers special **activities** for children, including games and sports.*

An *event* is something organised which people attend, usually a social gathering:
*The social **event** was a disaster – nobody came!*

These words are sometimes confused with *activity* or *event*:
- an *action* is the process of doing something or a physical movement:
  *He mimed the **actions** without saying a word.*
- a *happening* is an incident which may be difficult to explain, e.g. *a strange happening*
- a *meeting* is an event when people come together, often to discuss business
- an *organisation* is a group of people who work together for a common purpose:
  *The **organisation** holds monthly meetings.*
- a *programme* is a planned series of activities or events:
  *The school offers a **programme** of social events, including concerts and parties.*

2 Correct the mistake below.

For Herman, ...

3 Underline the correct words.

1 In my opinion, the *happening* / *event* was a big success.
2 Gymnastics is a popular sports *activity* / *event* at my school.
3 Everyone is invited to the next *activity* / *event*.
4 A *meeting* / *event* was held to discuss the club's finances.
5 The sports *organisation* / *event* was well attended.
6 The *organisation* / *event* is proud of the results.
7 The centre arranged a day of *activities* / *programmes* for older people.
8 We've organised a(n) *event* / *activity* / *programme* of events with activities to appeal
   to different people.

1 Are the sentences right or wrong? Correct those which are wrong.

1 Thank you for this occasion to speak to you tonight. ....

2 Do men and women in your country have equal possibilities? ....

3 He was given a second possibility to prove he could do the job. ....

4 I would like a job where there are chances for promotion. ....

5 Training possibilities are available for all members of staff. ....

6 All participants have the same possibility of winning. ....

7 He has a slim possibility of succeeding if he applies himself. ....

8 Don't miss this unique opportunity to see Picasso's later work. ....

2 Fill in the gaps with an appropriate word. Use *you, your, yours* or *you're*.

1 I'm sure .... going to be pleased.

2 I'd like to hear .... side of the story.

3 Thank you for .... concern.

4 I'll be waiting for .... at the station.

5 I've hung my jacket next to ....

6 I think this is .... biggest mistake.

7 Where do you think .... going?

8 Here's my bus – .... is number 30.

3 Complete the extract with a form of *activity, event, programme,* or *meeting*.

This season's coming (1) _____ include the Winter Street Festival, promising a packed (2) _____ of street theatre, music and dance. Another not-to-be-missed annual winter (3) _____ is the Historic Motor Sports Show. The (4) programme includes races, road rallies and speed events. A reminder for those 18-80s whose spare-time (5) activities range from bowling to ballroom dancing – the Social Club meets monthly on the first Tuesday of the month, 8.30 at the Rose and Crown. The December (6) _____ was very festive. The Club offers sport and social (7) _____ suitable for people of all ages. Finally, if you have a forthcoming (8) event which you would like to advertise, contact me on 01832-358217.

4 Circle the correct word for each space and complete the text.

Tips for improving (1) .... career

Here are seven ways to ensure (2) ....
ready to make the most of career (3) ....

1 Find a career mentor – someone to discuss
   (4) .... hopes and dreams with.
2 Understand what motivates (5) .... and
   be true to yourself. Make career decisions for yourself –
   the only career (6) .... can really
   influence is (7) ....
3 Be positive. If the boss notices, this will improve your
   (8) .... of promotion.
4 Grab any (9) .... to network, no matter
   how tired (10) .... feeling. Social
   (11) .... can be a great place to get
   yourself noticed.
5 Update (12) .... CV – and if
   (13) .... don't have an electronic
   version, get one.
6 Get noticed. Join a public or charitable
   (14) .... and attend meetings regularly.
7 Remember health and family. Take part in an
   (15) .... like tennis or swimming that
   will keep you fit. (16) .... expand
   when you are happy and healthy.

CV

1	you	your	yours	you're
2	you	your	yours	you're
3	possibilities	opportunities	chances	
4	you	your	yours	you're
5	you	your	yours	you're
6	you	your	yours	you're
7	you	your	yours	you're
8	possibilities	opportunities	chances	
9	possibilities	opportunities	chances	
10	you	your	yours	you're
11	events	activities	meetings	programmes
12	you	your	yours	you're
13	you	your	yours	you're
14	happening	activity	organisation	programme
15	event	activity	meeting	programme
16	Possibilities	Opportunities	Chances	

16 Commonly confused adjectives

1 Tick the correct sentence in each pair.

1 a There are free sport activities available to members.
  b There are free sports activities available to members.
2 a They have a varied range of healthy foods on offer.
  b They have a variety range of healthy foods on offer.

Sports, sporting or *sport*?
We can use *sports* and *sporting* as adjectives. *Sport* is a noun:
*Welcome to the school **sports day**. There are a number of **sporting events**.*
*What's your favourite **sport**? Do you play any **sports**?*
Common collocations with *sports* are *sports centre, sports club, sports day, sports competition, sports equipment, sports programme, sports teacher*

Open or *opened*?
We can use *open* as an adjective. *Opened* is a verb:
*We're **open** for business around the clock. The shop **opened** an hour ago.*

Varied or *variety*?
We can use *-ing* or *-ed* participles as adjectives:
*We offer a **varied** choice dishes.* (adj) *A **variety** of dishes is available.* (n)
***People** are **concerned** about the environment.* (adj) *The environment is a **concern**.* (n)
*When are you taking your **driving** test?* (adj) *Would you like to go for a **drive**?* (n)

Other forms which are confused are:
cultural (adj) / *culture* (n), *dramatic* (adj) / *dramatically* (adv), *true* (adj) / *truth* (n)

2 Correct the mistake below.

We're opened from 8 am to 10 pm.

fresh fish counter

We're ....

3 Are the underlined words right or wrong? Correct those which are wrong.

1 I'm <u>concern</u> about the transport strike. ....
2 Have you got a <u>driving</u> licence? ....
3 Everything we advertise is <u>truth</u>. ....
4 I have been <u>opened</u> about how I feel. ....
5 We organise <u>sport</u> events every month. ....
6 Life can take <u>dramatically</u> turns when you least expect it. ....
7 You should eat a <u>varied</u> of foods daily. ....
8 Hollywood has increased the <u>culture</u> influence of America. ....

Big, great or large?

1 Tick the correct sentence in each pair.

1. a We think our work here is of big importance.
   b We think our work here is of great importance.
2. a The choice of hot meals is too little.
   b The choice of hot meals is too limited.

Adjectives meaning *big* are used in these expressions:
- *great fun, of great importance, a great pleasure, a great success, a great variety*
- *a high level of something, high prices, a high standard (of living), high wages*
- *a large amount / number / quantity of something*
- *a wide choice / range / variety of something*

Adjectives meaning *little* are used in these expressions:
- *a limited choice of something, a limited / narrow range of something*
- *a small amount / number / quantity of something, a small business / firm*
- *a short break, a short holiday, a short time*
- *a low level of something, low pay / prices, a low standard (of living), low wages*

Also: *a minor problem, a light rain / shower*

Adjectives meaning *good, bad* or *wrong* are used in these expressions:
- *poor pay / wages, poor quality*
- *inadequate / insufficient leg room or space*
- *false / inaccurate information / figures / statement*

Also: *a bad habit, a positive response, a severe / serious illness*

2 Correct the mistake below.

> We're a little business, but we have plans to expand.

We're ....

3 Complete the sentences with an adjective meaning *big, little, good,* or *wrong*.

1. It's a .... pleasure to meet you.
2. We were paid a .... amount of money as a bonus.
3. There is a .... range of foods available.
4. We've worked hard. It's time for a .... break.
5. Thanks to a strong economy, we have a .... standard of living.
6. We don't need an umbrella – the forecast is for .... rain.
7. We have only a .... number of items left to sell.
8. It's a crime to give .... information to the police.

18 When do I use a hyphen in compound words?

1 Tick the correct sentence in each pair.

1 a The view from here is breath-taking.
  b The view from here is breathtaking.
2 a The newspaper is well known for its balanced coverage.
  b The newspaper is well-known for its balanced coverage.

We usually write compound adjectives with a hyphen:
above-mentioned, air-conditioned, all-inclusive, brand-new, English-speaking, easy-going, (five)-year-old, full-time, grown-up, living-room, middle-aged, middle-class. never-ending, self-centred, so-called, three-storey, top-class, well-known, well-paid

Some compound adjectives can be written as two words when used after the noun:
*It's a **top-class restaurant**. The **restaurant** is **top class**.*
*Anthony's a **well-known actor**. Anthony's **well known** as an actor.*

These compound words are usually written as one word:
breathtaking, hairdresser, lifestyle, lunchtime, worldwide:
*Football is a **worldwide sport**. Can you have this finished by **lunchtime**?*

These compound nouns are written as two words: *air conditioning, free time*. When they are used as adjectives they are hyphenated:
*What do you do in your **free time**?*
*She had to reduce her **free-time** activities when she started her new job.*

☆ If you are in doubt about whether a compound should be one word, two words or hyphenated, it is a good idea to consult a dictionary.

2 Correct the mistake below.

I'm sorry, Sir, but we don't serve breakfast dishes at lunch time.

I'm sorry, Sir, but ....

3 Are the sentences right or wrong? Correct those which are wrong.

1 The English language is spoken world wide. ....
2 The air-conditioning is too cold. Would you turn it down? ....
3 She goes to the hair-dresser once a week. ....
4 Moving to the country was a big life style change. ....
5 Could you make a note of the above-mentioned point? ....
6 Where are my so-called friends when I need them? ....
7 In my free-time, I watch television to relax. ....
8 The air-conditioning unit has broken down. ....

1 Are the sentences right or wrong? Correct those which are wrong.

1 His work as a medical researcher is of big importance. ....

2 In my country we eat a big quantity of pasta and bread. ....

3 The choice of dishes is little and the prices are high. ....

4 The pay for teachers and nurses in Britain is quite little. ....

5 The event was a good success and will doubtless take place again next year.
....

6 It's difficult to change wrong habits once they are formed. ....

7 I've decided to take a short holiday with my family. ....

8 The article wasn't carefully researched and contained wrong information.
....

2 Fill in the gaps with a suitable form of the words in the box. Use one word twice.

culture	concern	dramatic	open	truth	sport	vary

1 His work improved .... when he heard about his pay rise.

2 We're .... for business virtually round the clock.

3 Have you been to the new .... centre yet? They have an Olympic sized pool.

4 America has had a huge commercial and .... influence on the world.

5 People are increasingly .... about adopting a healthy lifestyle.

6 The new restaurant has healthy food, a .... menu and friendly staff.

7 Your advertisement sounds too good to be ....

8 Football is a popular .... with people of all ages.

3 Underline the correct form.

1 Her latest CD includes *brand new / brand-new* songs and recent hits.

2 She has three children but they're all *grown up / grown-up*.

3 I'm very *easy going / easy-going* and I love people.

4 He's *well known / well-known* for his love of fine art.

5 The view of the valley from our hotel room was *breathtaking / breath-taking*.

6 The club is popular with *middle aged / middle-aged* and older people.

7 Have you ever lived in an *English speaking / English-speaking* country?

8 I don't have a lot of *free time / free-time*, but I enjoy what I have.

4 Is each line in the extract below right or wrong? Correct those which are wrong.

1 Sports is an important part of the cultural tradition in Britain. Two

2 especially well liked national sports are football and tennis. For

3 football fans, nothing can compare with the excitement generated

4 every four-years by the World Cup, an event which is watched

5 virtually world-wide. The event is not only an opportunity to

6 watch top class football, it's also a chance to see some of the most

7 well known players in the world, celebrities in their own right. For

8 tennis lovers, Wimbledon, which takes place every June, is the event

9 to watch. This championship tennis competition is not only a sporting

10 event – it is a culture event. It is not uncommon for tennis lovers to

11 take a small holiday so that they can watch the matches undisturbed.

12 While some fans watch the games in the comfort of their living-rooms,

13 others are happy to brave the unpredictable June weather to watch

14 the games played live. There is some debate about whether the big

15 wages paid to professional sportspeople are excessive, but for many

16 fans, the big pleasure derived from watching a true professional in

action is worth any price.

1	....	9	....
2	....	10	....
3	....	11	....
4	....	12	....
5	....	13	....
6	....	14	....
7	....	15	....
8	....	16	....

Noun or verb?

Tick the correct sentence in each pair.

1 a Their main complain is related to the quality of the food.
    b Their main complaint is related to the quality of the food.

2 a Technology has greatly affected our lives.
    b Technology has greatly affected our lifes.

The verb *complain* and the noun *complaint* are often confused:
*Some people **are** always **complaining**.*
*We didn't hear any **complaints**.*

Other commonly confused forms are:

- *advise* (verb) and *advice* (noun):
  *It's better not to give **advice** to people who don't ask for it.*
- *live* (verb) and *life / lives* (noun):
  *This diet has changed my **life**.*
- *sit / sat* (verb) and *seat* (noun):
  *Could we have **seats** at the front of the cinema, please?* (not *could we have sits*)
- *pay / paid* (verb) and *payment* (noun):
  *Which method of **payment** do you prefer – cash or credit card?* (not *method of paying*)
- *stay* (verb) and *stay* (noun):
  *I hope you enjoy your **stay** in Britain.* (not *your staying*)

2 Correct the mistake below.

My advise to you is to be very tolerant.

My ....

Underline the correct word.

1 What's the most frequent *complain / complaint* you receive from students?
2 Mainly, they *complain / complaint* that there are too many students in the class.
3 Change is inevitable – you've come to a turning point in your *life / live*.
4 How would you like to be *pay / paid* for your work – cash or cheque?
5 When we go to the theatre, we buy the best *sits / seats* we can afford.
6 A good piece of *advice / advise* is, 'Don't worry!'
7 Unfortunately, every business will receive its share of *complains / complaints*.
8 Jenny enjoyed her *stay / staying* in America, but was glad to get home.

How do I use negative prefixes?

1 Tick the correct sentence in each pair.

1 a The coach driver was very unpolite and unfriendly.
  b The coach driver was very impolite and unfriendly.
2 a In fact, the whole tour was quite dissatisfactory.
  b In fact, the whole tour was quite unsatisfactory.

These prefixes give words a negative meaning: *un-, in-, im-, dis-, mis-* and *non-*.

The most common negative prefix is <u>*un-*</u>. Some words taking *un-* are:
unavailable, uncomfortable, unconditional, unconscious, unconvincing, undemanding, undoubtedly, unforgettable, unforgivable, unlimited, unnecessary, unoccupied, unpolluted, unprejudiced, unsatisfactory, unscheduled

in- is also a commonly-used prefix. Words taking *in-* are:
inadequate, inadvisable, inappropriate, incapable, incompetent, incomplete, inconvenient, ineffective, inexcusable, inexpensive, inexperienced, insecure, insufficient, intolerable

We use *im-* before words beginning with *p* and *m*:
impolite, impossible, impractical, improper, immature

Words taking *non-* are: *non-existent, non-native*
Words taking *mis-* are: *mislead, misunderstand*
Words taking *dis-* are: *discourage, disobedient, disorganised, dissatisfied*
☆ We say ***un**satisfactory* (adj), but ***dis**satisfaction* (noun) and ***dis**satisfied* (adj).

2 Correct the mistake below.

Actually, I'm looking for something unexpensive.

Actually, ...

3 Complete each sentence with a negative form of the word in brackets.

1 The College canteen is .... and needs to be improved. *(adequate)*
2 You .... my meaning or you wouldn't have taken offence.
  (understand)
3 I don't accept that my behaviour was in any way .... *(proper)*
4 I'm writing to express my .... with your firm. *(satisfy)*
5 We're most unhappy with the .... service you provided. *(satisfy)*
6 I'm afraid your report is .... *(complete)*
7 For a .... speaker, your pronunciation is excellent. *(native)*
8 Thank you for a(n) .... holiday. *(forget)*

When do I use *regarding*?

21

1 Tick the correct sentence in each pair.

1 a That's all I have to say as for myself.

  b ✓ That's all I have to say regarding myself.

2 a ✓ According to the *Financial Times*, that company is facing bankruptcy.

  b Regarding the *Financial Times*, that company is facing bankruptcy.

In a more formal context, we use *regarding* + noun to introduce a new idea or topic.
Regarding your visit on Thursday, I wonder if you could arrive after 10.00.

Other expressions used in this way are *as regards* and *as for*. *As regards* often indicates a change of topic:
The food for the event has been organised. However, as regards the entertainment …

As for may indicate a negative attitude on the part of the speaker:
As for the schedule, it could be difficult to manage.

☆ We use *according to* + noun, not *regarding*, to mean 'as stated by':
According to the Prime Minister, the economy continues to improve.

☆ We use *in my opinion*, but not *according to me* to state our own opinion.

When *regarding* occurs mid-sentence, it often replaces the preposition *about*:
I am writing to you regarding / about your choice of accommodation.

Regarding can also partner words in place of *in*, *of* and *on*:
We've made remarkable progress regarding / in customer relations.
What are your expectations regarding / of the team?
Ten years ago, these regulations regarding / on working conditions did not exist.

2 Correct the mistake below.

Sir, I'd like to speak to you as regards a pay rise.

Manager

Sir, ...

3 Are the sentences right or wrong? Correct those which are wrong.

1 About the hotel, it was much too far from the train station. ....

2 As regarding the entertainment, I found it to be excellent. ....

3 According to the variety of food, there will be dishes for vegetarians. ....

4 For these complaints, we need to decide what action to take. ....

5 The government is quite concerned about this matter. ....

6 I'll give you my advice as for passing your driving test. ....

7 In the new clubroom, we could paint it yellow. ....

8 We've made remarkable progress in medical science. ....

TEST 7

1 Complete the sentences with an appropriate form of the word in brackets.

1 The child was punished for her ....(obey)

2 We were promised a(n) .... holiday and we did have a wonderful time. (forget)

3 Employment opportunities in this part of the country are practically
.... (exist)

4 Your desk looks so .... – can't you tidy it up? (organise)

5 .... love for another person is perhaps something only parents feel. (condition)

6 The barrister's arguments were too .... to sway the opinion of the jury. (convince)

7 I'd love to own a sports car, but it would be .... with a large family. (practical)

8 Many people in the world are forced to live in conditions others would find
.... (tolerate)

2 Underline the correct form.

1 I'd *advice / advise* you to be careful about who you confide in.

2 Millions of people lost their *lives / lifes* in the Second World War.

3 I'm concerned about the current situation *of / regarding* our work efficiency.

4 We were presented with a list of *complains / complaints* about the product.

5 Our three day *stay / staying* in Paris was just the break we needed.

6 We'd have enjoyed the performance more if we'd had better *sits / seats.*

7 *About / Regarding* diet and accommodation, do you have any special requirements?

8 I think the *paying / payment* for my work should be increased.

3 Are the sentences right or wrong? Where necessary, change the sentence using *regarding*.

1 I'd like to speak to you about your proposal for a training programme.
....

2 I'd be pleased to give you my advice for improvements to the College. ....

3 I am writing to express my dissatisfaction for the tour. ....

4 About public transport, future developments have been planned. ....

5 I'm a little concerned about some points of the organisation of the tour.
....

6 According to the Production Manager, productivity has increased this month.
....

7 For your request for more office equipment, I'm afraid it has been refused.
....

8 About the danger of a transport strike, negotiations are underway. ....

4 Read the notes and, using the information given, complete the letter of complaint. Write the missing words in the space provided. Use only one word in each space.

Bus too small – nowhere to sit
Bus made stops not on schedule
Rooms dirty and not comfortable
Waiters not polite or organised
Wouldn't accept payment by cheque
Location not convenient – 4 miles from town centre

I am writing on behalf of my firm to make a (1) .... regarding the service your hotel provided at our annual convention. Firstly, the bus which transported us from the train station to the hotel did not have enough (2) .... and as a result many delegates were forced to stand. Moreover, the driver made two (3) .... stops. When we finally arrived at the hotel, we found our rooms dirty and (4) .... Later, we had dinner in your restaurant. The food was tasty but the waiter was (5) .... and (6) .... In fact, when the bill was presented he wouldn't accept a cheque and insisted we should (7) .... by cash or credit card. Finally, you described the location of your hotel as 'central' when, in fact, it was located four miles from the centre, which was most (8) .... I look forward to receiving a letter of apology and an offer of compensation.

5 Fill in the gaps with a form of the words in the box.

comfort	conscious	depend	lead
patient	success	understand	verbal

Body Language

Understanding body language can teach us a great deal about human behaviour.

Much research has been done into whether (1) .... signals are inborn or learnt, and experiments have shown that the smiling expressions of children born deaf and blind occur (2) .... of learning. Do you cross your arms left over right or right over left? Most people will find that where one way feels good, the other feels very (3) .... It seems that basic communication gestures are the same worldwide. However, cultural differences in body language, gesture in particular, can cause (4) ...., and these can be highly embarrassing.

Much of what we communicate through body language is done (5) .... That is to say, we are unaware of the message we are conveying. Is it possible, then, to fake body language so as to deliberately (6) .... others? Skilled communicators, like actors or politicians may do so for short periods of time, but your average person would be (7) .... even at this. If you want to learn to read body language, go to an airport – here you can observe a spectrum of gestures as people openly express anger, sorrow, (8) .... and many other emotions.

22 How do I punctuate sentences with *because* and *however*?

1 Tick the correct sentence in each pair.

1 a Because she was driving too quickly she skidded and nearly had an accident.
   b Because she was driving too quickly, she skidded and nearly had an accident.

2 a I want to learn English, however lots of people in my class don't feel that way.
   b I want to learn English. However, lots of people in my class don't feel that way.

However is an adverb. We use *however*:
- to highlight a contrast with the idea in the previous sentence
- to start a new sentence. *However* is followed by a comma:
  The cost was advertised as all-inclusive. **However**, *we had to pay for meals.*

Nevertheless is used in a similar way to *however*, but is more formal.

Because is a conjunction. We use *because*:
- to give a reason for the situation or event in the main clause.
- to link two clauses. The clause with *because* usually comes after the main clause. When it comes first, it is followed by a comma.
  We were unhappy with the service **because** *we had to pay for meals.*
  Because *we had to pay for meals, we were unhappy with the service.*

As and *since* are also conjunctions which can be used to introduce a reason. Clauses with *as* or *since* often come at the beginning of the sentence:
As it was nearly one o'clock, we decided to break for lunch.

2 Correct the mistake below.

I'm afraid I won't be able to come to your party. Because I'm going away that weekend.

I'm afraid ....

3 Join the sentences using *however* or *because*. Use capital letters and / or commas where necessary.

1 I'd like a refund. I'm dissatisfied with the service you provided. ....
2 We provide vegetarian food. There is an extra charge for this. ....
3 I'd like to accept the job. There are some points I need to clarify. ....
4 There was a thunderstorm. I arrived at College wet and cold. ....
5 We visited a beautiful cathedral. That was the only enjoyable part of the holiday.
   ....
6 This is one solution to the problem. There are other solutions. ....
7 We think the canteen is unhygienic. We are refusing to eat there ....
8 Suzanne's feeling very irritable. She's tired. ....

How do I use *because of*?

1 Tick the correct sentence in each pair.

1 a Our lives have changed a lot because of new technology.

  b Our lives have changed a lot by new technology.

2 a I would like to thank you for your invitation.

  b I would like to thank you because of your invitation.

Because of or *because*?
Because of is a two-word preposition. We use *because of* + a noun or a pronoun:
*I can't live in a house with pets **because of an allergy**.*

Because is a conjunction. We use *because* + a clause:
*I can't live in a house with pets **because I have an allergy**.*

Because of, *for*, or *by*?
We use *because of* + noun to show the cause of a situation or event. *Owing to* and *due to* can be used in the same way:
*They were delayed **because of** / **owing to** / **due to** bad weather.*
☆ We can use *due to*, but not *because of* or *owing to*, after the verb *to be*:
*His wealth **is due to** his lottery win.*

We use *for* + noun to introduce an explanation for our behaviour:
*I'd like to thank you **for the time you gave me**.*

We use *by* + noun in a passive construction to show the agent or cause of an action:
*We were misled **by your advertisement**.*

2 Correct the mistake below.

James is off school for illness.

James ....

3 Underline the correct words.

1 The firm closed down last month *for* / *because of* financial problems.
2 *Because* / *Because of* the money I earn, I'm able to help others.
3 John is feeling stressed *for* / *because of* a hectic job.
4 I'm not happy with the tour *for* / *because of* two reasons.
5 The garden furniture was destroyed *by* / *because of* pouring rain.
6 Sales are suffering *for* / *because of* a lack of a committed sales team.
7 You were recommended *because* / *because of* you offer top-quality service.
8 The storm damage was *owing to* / *due to* the exceptionally high winds.

41

24 If or whether?

1 Tick the correct sentence in each pair.

1 a   I think it would be better whether the tour went ahead as planned.
  b   I think it would be better if the tour went ahead as planned.
2 a   The question was about whether I agreed with the proposal.
  b   The question was about if I agreed with the proposal.

We can use the conjunctions *if* and *whether*:

* in reported *yes* / *no* questions:
  *She asked me **if** / **whether** I would take the job she offered me.*
* after expressions like *I'm not sure, I don't know*, and *I wonder*:
  *I'm not sure **if** / **whether** I should answer your question.*
* in expressions with *or not*:
  *I want to know **if** / **whether** you're coming to the event **or not**.*

Only *whether* is possible:

* in the expression *whether or not*:
  *I want to know **whether or not** you're coming to the event.*
* after prepositions:
  *I was worried **about whether** something had happened to her.*

Only *if* is possible in conditional sentences:
If you're not interested in the idea, you should say so.

☆ *Even if* introduces a condition, while *even though* is similar in meaning to *although*.
When the clauses with *if* and *even if* come first, they are followed by a comma.
***Even if** I win the lottery, I won't give up work.*

2 Correct the mistake below.

Go on. Talk to her and see if or not you like her.

Go on. Talk to her ....

3 Complete the sentences with *if* or *whether*. In some sentences both are possible.

1 We should ask them .... the accommodation is all right.
2 Janice was worried about .... she had passed the exam or not.
3 Even .... I knew I'd get away with it, I wouldn't cheat in an exam.
4 I get very irritable .... I don't get enough sleep.
5 We may be late. It depends on .... the train is delayed.
6 I want to know .... there is any chance of getting my money back.
7 We'd like to know .... or not you are pleased with our service.
8 I'm not sure .... accepting the job would be a good idea.

1 **Are the sentences right or wrong? Correct those which are wrong.**

1 I'd like a refund of forty pounds because my dissatisfaction with the product.
....

2 Owing to the late arrival of the train, we were late for our appointment.
....

3 I chose the driving school by the pass rates of the people who went there.
....

4 The car is in poor condition because of it hasn't been well-maintained.
....

5 She was frightened because of the dogs. ....

6 I would like to thank you because of your invitation to take part in this event.
....

7 I hesitated to tell you what had happened because of many reasons. ....

8 Our meetings will be more successful because of your help. ....

2 **Correct any mistakes in punctuation. Add capital letters where necessary.**

1 In some countries a bride can't see the groom the night before the wedding because it's considered bad luck. ....

2 The Party Conference ended successfully however a lot of issues were not discussed.
....

3 Because he was feeling unwell he decided not to attend the meeting. ....

4 I used to keep fit however I've been too busy of late to do so. ....

5 We arrived late because of the heavy traffic. ....

6 Due to the difficulties the firm experienced they had to close down. ....

7 If you want to see the beginning of the film you'll have to hurry. ....

8 Don't make a decision now just because I said you should. ....

3 **Underline the correct words.**

1 Even *if / though* we couldn't manage without their help, I wouldn't ask them.

2 I think it would be better *if / whether* the sightseeing tour were cancelled.

3 I'm still not sure about *if / whether* to accept the job or not.

4 I'd like to know *if / whether* or not you agree with my suggestions.

5 They didn't take care of me even *if / though* I was ill.

6 *If / Whether* you hadn't lied about your age, we wouldn't be in this situation.

7 *If / Although* the classrooms are excellent, the food in the canteen is terrible.

8 I'd like to arrange a meeting *if / whether* you think that's convenient.

4 Complete the extract by writing an appropriate linking expression in the space provided. Use one or two words for each space.

How to make decisions

Making decisions is a practical matter. (1) .... there is enough information to make the decision for us, then we, as humans, are unnecessary. It is only necessary, then, to make decisions when we have to speculate or guess (2) .... the analysis of the information is insufficient. Some decisions are simple to make (3) .... the correctness of the decision can be checked immediately. (4) .... , the difficulty is usually that the correctness of the decision can only be checked in the future – after we've made the decision.

Before making a decision we must think about the situation in which it is to be made. For example, we need to decide (5) .... there is a need to make a decision at all and (6) .... or not it's necessary to make the decision now. What will happen (7) .... the decision is put off? When questions like these are answered, one acceptable method of making a decision is simply to throw a die. (8) .... this seems irrational, there is quite a lot of sense to it. This is (9) .... psychologists have discovered that people tend to get to like decisions after they have been made. So (10) .... you're uncertain about (11) .... to choose one alternative or another, let 'someone else' decide and then see (12) .... you would be happy with that decision.

(13) .... , decisions not only have to be made but they also have to be acted upon. The 'easy way out' method suggests we choose the easiest alternative to carry out. Of course, (14) .... differences in personality, the 'easiest' method will differ from person to person. Once the choice has been made, make the effort to justify the decision. (15) .... , at the end of this effort, the choice still seems acceptable, then the decision can be made. (16) .... not, then some other decision method is needed.

44

How do I use *put*?

1 Tick the correct sentence in each pair.

1 a Things go missing when you don't put them in the right place.

  b Things go missing when you don't put them on the right place.

2 a The work we put in this event was worth it.

  b The work we put into this event was worth it.

We *put on (something)* we wear:
*She has to **put on a wig** / **put a wig on** for her part in the play.*

We *put up (something)* we are hanging, e.g. on a wall:
*I **put up the curtains** / **put the curtains up** in the bedroom.*

We *put (something)* in the right place.

We *put in work* or *effort*:
*I **put in** a lot of **effort** / **put** a lot of **effort in** when I decide to do something.*

We *put work / effort / enthusiasm into (something)*:
*He **put** a lot of **work into preparing** for his exams.*

We *put (something) into practice*:
*You need to **put what you've learnt in class into practice** / **put into practice what you've learnt**.*

When we *put forward something* we offer or suggest it, e.g. *put forward an idea / put an idea forward*.

Put on (something) can mean 'to provide it', e.g. ***put on a performance***.

2 Correct the mistake below.

Can you put the posters and I'll post the leaflets?

Can you .... ?

3 Insert an appropriate preposition.

1 I try to put enthusiasm everything I do. ....

2 We put a lot of work when preparing for the party. ....

3 The amount of work we put this event should be appreciated. ....

4 It's time you put your ideas practice. ....

5 The show was so popular the troupe decided to put an extra performance. ....

6 Would you put these pictures for me, please? ....

7 Why are you putting your coat? Are you ready to leave? ....

8 Could you put that the right place – where it belongs? ....

26 Pay or spend?

1 Tick the correct sentence in each pair.

1. a   I'd appreciate it if the firm paid for my expenses as soon as possible.
   b   I'd appreciate it if the firm paid my expenses as soon as possible.
2. a   The government has spent a lot of money in the construction of roads.
   b   The government has spent a lot of money on the construction of roads.

Pay (for) (something)
When we purchase something which then becomes ours, we *pay for* the item:
*Breakfast was included, but we **paid for** our other meals.*

When we *pay (something)* because the money is owed, we omit *for*, e.g. *pay a bill*:
*We **paid the bill** with cash. Don't forget to **pay the rent**.*

Spend money and *time*
We *spend money on (something)*:
*Young people **spend a lot of money on entertainment**.*

We *spend time (doing something)*:
*We **spent the afternoon sitting in the garden**.*

We *spend time* + preposition + place:
- *spend time at* a building or location, e.g. *at a theatre / castle, at the beach*
- *spend time in* a city or country, e.g. *in London / Canada*
- *spend time in* an enclosed area, e.g. *in the garden / bath / swimming pool*
- *spend time with (someone)*, e.g. *with a friend*
  *We **spent an afternoon at the beach**. We **spent eight days in London with my parents**.*

2 Correct the mistake below.

The holiday? We spent most of our time in shopping.

We spent ....

3 Are these sentences right or wrong? Correct those which are wrong.

1. All our expenses were paid by the company. ....
2. They paid all our meals and our accommodation. ....
3. How much time do you spend doing your homework? ....
4. How long did you spend at Madrid? ....
5. How did you pay the tickets – cash or credit card? ....
6. The evening we spent in the theatre was terrible. ....
7. How much money did you spend for the holiday? ....
8. I spent the weekend in my family. ....

Which preposition do I use?

1 **Tick the correct sentence in each pair.**

1 a   He just needs someone to pay attention on him.

    b   He just needs someone to pay attention to him.

2 a   The article of your magazine is quite interesting.

    b   The article in your magazine is quite interesting.

There are many examples of dependent prepositions in English:

Verb + preposition:
- *care for (something)* or *(someone)*, e.g. *care for a child / an animal*
- *draw / pay attention to (something)*, e.g. *draw attention to a problem, pay attention to a teacher*

Preposition + noun:
- *in* a publication, e.g. *to publish something in a newspaper*
- *in my opinion, in conclusion*

Noun + preposition:
- *an expert in (something)*, e.g. *an expert in tropical diseases*
- *the purpose of (something)*, e.g. *the purpose of the research*
- *(a) reason(s) for (something)*, e.g. *a reason for a political change*
- *(dis)satisfaction with (something)*, e.g. *dissatisfaction with service*

Adjective + preposition:
- *responsible for (something)*, e.g. *responsible for a mistake*
- *interested in (something)*, e.g. *interested in learning a language*

2 **Correct the mistake below.**

May I draw your attention on the graph, please?

May I .... ?

3 **Underline the correct word.**

1 Thank you for paying attention *about / to* my letter.

2 The advertisement was printed *in / on* magazines throughout Britain.

3 I write to draw your attention *on / to* the article in your newspaper.

4 A nurse's job is to care *about / for* patients, even when she dislikes them.

5 I wonder if you could you tell me the reasons *about / for* your decision?

6 It takes years to become an expert *at / in* a subject.

7 I am writing in response to the article which appeared *at / in* the *Times*.

8 I can't help feeling responsible *about / for* what's gone wrong.

1 Are the sentences right or wrong? Correct those which are wrong.

1 The visitor centre is the place to pay for your entrance fee. ....

2 I'd like to express my dissatisfaction about the service we received. ....

3 Could I draw your attention to the information in Figure 3? ....

4 When you're driving, you must pay attention on the traffic. ....

5 I'm sorry, but I feel responsible about what has gone wrong. ....

6 How much effort did you really put in preparing for your exams? ....

7 I'm interested about knowing more about what your firm can offer. ....

8 People generally spend a large proportion of their income for rent. ....

2 Complete the sentence with a preposition.

1 I trained for two years to learn how to care .... young children.

2 If I'd paid more attention .... my teachers, I'd have got better marks.

3 I think you'd better put .... a heavier coat – it's cold outside.

4 The main purpose .... learning a language is communication.

5 What an afternoon! I spent most of it .... the dentist's!

6 I was disgusted by the article which appeared .... last month's publication.

7 Please let me pay .... lunch. It's my turn.

8 Edward is an expert .... early childhood development.

3 Is each line in the email below right or wrong? Correct those which are wrong. There may be a word missing or a wrong word.

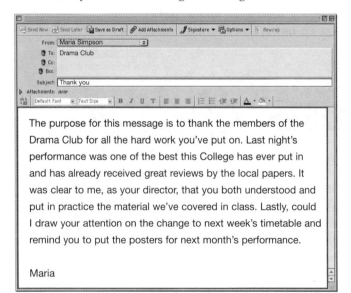

4 Complete the extract by writing the missing words in the space provided. Use only one word in each space. Sometimes no word is needed.

Personal debt on the rise

The report published (1) .... last week's edition of the *Standard* looks at trends in spending. Firstly, the report draws attention (2) .... the sharp increase in personal debt. The average person today is £5,330 in debt compared with £3,540 in 1997 according to the Office of National Statistics, a rise of over 50%. The average income, on the other hand, has risen by only 23.5% in the same period, from £12,400 to £15,310. The report puts (3) .... the suggestion that an increase in consumer spending is responsible (4) .... the increase in debt. The report suggests that while the average person will spend their money (5) .... consumer products, they are not interested (6) .... paying (7) .... financial services which contribute to savings. One reason given (8) .... this lack of interest in saving for a rainy day is low interest rates, which also makes borrowing easier. Advice for consumers is to keep track of how much they spend (9) .... bills, at the supermarket, etc., and to pay (10) .... credit card bills promptly.

5 Complete the second sentence so that it means the same as the first sentence, using the words in brackets. Use between two and five words.

1 Have you paid for the meal yet? *(bill)*
   Have you .... yet?
2 Young people should take notice of what their parents suggest. *(attention)*
   Young people .... their parents.
3 Would anybody like to make a suggestion? *(forward)*
   Would anybody .... a suggestion?
4 I'd like you now to consider Section 2 of the report. *(attention)*
   I'd like to .... Section 2 of the report.
5 The time for you to act on your ideas is now. *(practice)*
   The time for you to .... is now.
6 Food costs our family a lot of money. *(spend)*
   Our family .... food.

49

What are some common spelling mistakes?

1 **Tick the correct sentence in each pair.**

1 a This is an opportunity we can't afford to miss.
  b This is an oportunity we can't afford to miss.
2 a I'm writing with reference to the holiday accomodation you provided.
  b I'm writing with reference to the holiday accommodation you provided.

Many English words are spelt differently than they sound. Words may be misspelt because they have:

- double letters:
  *acco**mm**odation, busine**ss**, reco**mm**end, o**pp**ortunity, disa**pp**ointment /-ed /-ing, co**mm**i**tt**ee, nece**ss**ary, di**ff**erent, profe**ss**ional*
- silent letters:
  *colleag**u**es, environ**m**ent, **k**now, nig**h**t*
- letters which are difficult to predict from the sound:
  choice, comfortable, grammar, negotiate

Be careful not to add or leave out letters. These words are also commonly misspelt:
according, addition, afraid, apartment, attractive, career, exaggerated, intelligent, millennium, until

2 **Correct the mistake below.**

Open ....

3 **Underline the correct spelling of the word.**

1 Which would you *reccommend / recommend* – the fish or the steak?
2 The *environment / enviroment* is a major concern for many people.
3 Do whatever you think is *necessary / nessecary* to solve the problem.
4 The *committee / commitee* is meeting next Monday. Will you be there?
5 I've gone back to College. It's time for a *carreer / career* change.
6 Your exam results are *disappointing / dissappointing*. What happened?
7 I really enjoy working with my *collegues / colleagues*.
8 The news reports of the conflict *exaggerated / exagerated* the casualties.

Is the spelling British or American?

1 Tick the British English spelling in each pair.

1 a How often do you practise playing the piano?
  b How often do you practice playing the piano?
2 a We'd planned to go to the theater, but the performance was cancelled.
  b We'd planned to go to the theatre, but the performance was cancelled.

The British and American spellings of many English words are different. While both spellings are equally correct, British English and British spellings are preferred in the Cambridge examinations. Some areas of difference are:

- words ending in *-re* or *-er*
  British English prefers: *centre, theatre, metre* (but *gas* or *parking meter*)
  American English prefers: *center, theater, meter.*

- words ending in *-se* or *-ce*
  British spelling prefers: *practice (n) / practise (v), licence (n) / license (v)*
  American spelling prefers: *practice, licence (n and v)*

- words ending in *-our* or *-or*
  British spelling prefers: *behaviour, colour, humour, labour, neighbour, rumour*
  American spelling prefers: *behavior, color, humor, labor, neighbor, rumor*

Note these differences:
cheque (UK), check (USA)   programme (UK), program (USA)
☆ We say *computer program* in British English.

2 Correct the mistakes below.

welcome.
We are not
licenced to
serve alcohol.
Checks not
accepted.

We are ....

3 Change the underlined word to British spelling where necessary.

1 What color is your new car? ....
2 Is it all right if I write you a check, or would you like cash? ....
3 The traffic in the center of town is terrible this time of day. ....
4 I haven't met our new neighbor yet. Have you? ....
5 I missed football practice this morning. I wasn't well. ....
6 I hate quiz programs. Could we change the channel? ....
7 Come and have a look. I've installed a new program in my computer. ....
8 Do you think British humor is very different from American humor? ....

30 Kids or children?

1 Tick the correct sentence in each pair.

1 a Many women don't stay at home with their kids, but seek work instead.
  b Many women don't stay at home with their children, but seek work instead.
2 a Many people are gonna change their lifestyle as a result of recent research.
  b Many people are going to change their lifestyle as a result of recent research.

The register of written language is generally more formal than the register of spoken language. Some features of spoken English are:

- the use of slang in place of more neutral or formal equivalents: *children → kids, money → dosh or bread, police officer → cop(per), fool → prat or wally, toilet → loo, friend → mate, pound(s) → quid, bacteria or virus → bug, thick → stupid*

  ☆ It is helpful to understand slang expressions, but it can be difficult to identify an appropriate context for using such expressions. Also, be warned that slang expressions date and can easily sound old-fashioned.

- *can* for *could* in requests for permission
- *Do you want to …?* for *Would you like to …?* in invitations
- the use of 'shortened' expressions like *gonna* for 'going to' and *wanna* for 'want to'
- the use of contractions: *I'm, he's, hasn't*
- the use of phrasal verbs: *put up with* for *tolerate, find out* for *discover*

The language we use for public purposes, e.g. in work or study, is usually more formal. Language we use for personal purposes, i.e. with family and friends, is usually less formal. For this reason, spoken language which we use in a public context, e.g. a speech or an examination, contains the features of more formal written language.

2 Correct the mistake below.

I'd like to speak to a cop, please.

I'd ....

3 Change the underlined word to a more formal equivalent.

1 I have had a lot of experience looking after <u>kids</u> of all ages. ....
2 I beg your pardon. Could you tell me where the <u>loo</u> is, please? ....
3 We were advised to invest our <u>dosh</u> in a high interest savings account. ....
4 Your illness has been caused by a highly infectious <u>bug</u>. ....
5 We must consider how we're <u>gonna</u> meet the demands of the coming year. ....
6 I wonder if you could lend me ten <u>quid</u> until tomorrow, please? ....
7 Shall we ask that <u>cop</u> for directions? ....
8 He's a respected politician and also a close <u>mate</u> of the family. ....

Find and correct the mistakes in spelling.

1 Accomodation in any major city is prohibitively expensive. ....

2 Can you recomend a reasonably-priced restaurant nearby? ....

3 I'm afraid I don't feel confortable with that decision. ....

4 The members of this commitee all work voluntarily. ....

5 Running your own bussiness takes a great deal of commitment. ....

6 I have been offered an atractive opportunity to work abroad. ....

7 Do you think proffesional athletes make too much money? ....

8 Although they're twins, their personalities are quite diferent. ....

Underline the British spelling of the words in italics.

1 Would you give me the measurements in *meters / metres*, please?

2 He was arrested for threatening *behaviour / behavior*.

3 How can you expect to improve at anything if you don't *practice / practise*?

4 My favourite television *programs / programmes* are all soaps.

5 Who are the *favourites / favorites* to win the match?

6 Who should this *cheque / check* be payable to?

7 As an actress she prefers *theater / theatre* work to films.

8 He worked for many years as a farm *labourer / laborer*.

Is each line in the extract below right or wrong? Correct those which are wrong.

1	The two main political parties in Britain are Labor and Conservative,
2	sometimes known as the Tories. While the former usually shows more
3	concern for issues like education, healthcare and the enviroment, many
4	people who voted for the present goverment have not been happy with their
5	policies to date. Many traditional supporters have been dissapointed that so
6	little appears to have been done to improve public services. Choises have to
7	be made, yet many voters still feel that precious oportunities to make
8	nessecary changes to the infrastructure of the country have been lost.

1 ....   5 ....

2 ....   6 ....

3 ....   7 ....

4 ....   8 ....

4 Read the extract from a composition and replace the words in italics with more formal or neutral equivalents.

A career choice is one of the most important decisions made in life. My sister is a teacher, and she insists that it is a career you should choose only if you genuinely enjoy the company of (1) .... *(kids)*. Sometimes she thinks she was (2) .... *(thick)* to choose a job where she works very long hours for so little (3) .... *(dosh)*, but on the whole I think she's happy with her choice. My brother, on the other hand, is a (4) .... *(copper)*. He risks his life for twenty thousand (5) .... *(quid)* a year and has to (6) .... *(put up with)* people who behave like (7) .... *(prats)*. Still, he doesn't complain either. He maintains he's made some great (8) .... *(mates)* in the police force and, like my sister, he gets a great deal of satisfaction out of helping people.

5 Complete the rest of the missing words. Use British spelling.

1 Have you met the new *ne*..*rs* yet? They moved in last week.

2 Was 2000 or 2001 the beginning of the *mi*..*um*?

3 He has a tendency to *ex*..*ate* the importance of his work.

4 *Ac*..*ing* to recent figures, there has been a fall in unemployment.

5 I am lucky to work with very supportive *co*..*gues*.

6 Unless I can *ne*.. *ate* a pay rise, I will have to look for another job.

7 As the job market changes, people are forced to adapt by changing *ca*..*rs*.

8 There's a *ru*..*r* circulating that there will be job losses in our department.

Answer key

Unit 1
1 1 b
   2 b
2 been writing this essay
3 1 've lived
   2 've been attending
   3 'd been driving
   4 haven't taken
   5 'd worked
   6 's changed
   7 've been working
   8 's always taken

Unit 2
1 1 a
   2 b
2 has been
3 1 has improved
   2 was invented
   3 applied
   4 had been left
   5 has changed
   6 has been proved
   7 have organised
   8 handed in

Unit 3
1 1 a
   2 b
2 having a barbecue
3 1 Have you had
   2 We had
   3 Maria gives
   4 were given
   5 has had
   6 Are we having
   7 can have
   8 'll give

Test 1
1 1 gives, speech
   2 have, appointment
   3 had, problems
   4 give, explanation
   5 have, idea
   6 had, experience; give, advice
2 1 have you been doing

   2 I've been working
   3 I've had
   4 I've been teaching
   5 I've always wanted
   6 I've been thinking
   7 I've heard
   8 Have you seen
   9 I haven't been
   10 Have you rung
3 1 were issued / given out
   2 was obtained / achieved
   3 have been made
   4 has been decided
   5 was scheduled / had been scheduled
   6 has been postponed
4 1 have been reported
   2 have surrounded
   3 has been taking place
   4 has announced
   5 has been given
   6 had denied
   7 have been building
   8 has been
   9 have been
   10 has virtually come
5 1 were announced
   2 We had
   3 It's been raining
   4 agreed to give me
   5 *correct*
   6 *correct*
   7 was made

Unit 4
1 1 b
   2 b
2 to tell you about my experiences working for a large multinational
3 1 give you my word
   2 *correct*
   3 sent her a message / sent a message to her
   4 give you some advice
   5 for telling me / us / them about
   6 told the police the truth / told the truth to the police

7 told me / them / us where
8 *correct*

Unit 5
1 1 a
  2 b
2 I have to ask you to leave, Sir
3 1 to change
  2 to travel
  3 taking
  4 make
  5 to consider
  6 do
  7 playing
  8 feeling

Unit 6
1 1 b
  2 a
2 offer individual tuition
3 1 provide
  2 offer
  3 provided
  4 offering
  5 provide
  6 offer / give
  7 given
  8 give

Test 2
1 1 provides
  2 provide
  3 offered
  4 give
  5 provide
  6 offering
  7 offer
  8 offering
2 1 with
  2 —
  3 you
  4 for
  5 us / me
  6 me
  7 —
  8 us / me
3 1 *correct*
  2 provide / provide you with / offer you

3 offer you
4 send us confirmation
5 *correct*
6 inform us in advance
7 provide you with
8 assure you of
4 1 forced him to go on a strict diet
  2 authorised him to take unpaid leave from work
  3 ask you to do something for me
  4 not to allow him to take the exam
  5 prevented witnesses (from) leaving the scene of the crime
  6 made me sign the document
  7 get my computer to work no matter what I do
  8 assured me they would help in any way they could
5 1 *correct*
  2 allow me to go out
  3 smell food cooking
  4 children to stay up past
  5 told me why
  6 *correct*
  7 passengers to go
  8 prevents him (from) working

Unit 7
1 1 b
  2 b
2 he had to stay at home yesterday, as well
3 1 must be / must have been
  2 mustn't argue
  3 must have eaten
  4 had to go
  5 can't be
  6 must be
  7 didn't have to buy
  8 can't have told

Unit 8
1 1 a
  2 b
2 will never improve if you don't practise
3 1 can still live well
  2 might even have come first

3 I'd have happily agreed / I'd happily have agreed
4 can only see it
5 can also be very expensive
6 I definitely can't go out
7 could you possibly go ahead
8 shouldn't ever drink

Unit 9

1 1 b
2 b
2 was supposed to be here an hour ago
3 1 are supposed to
2 was supposed to
3 meant
4 are we expected
5 was meant
6 supposed to
7 was expected
8 were supposed

Test 3

1 1 meals are meant to be
2 *correct*
3 *correct*
4 cats are supposed to be
5 *correct*
6 Technology is meant to
7 You're expected to
8 You're supposed to
2 1 're supposed to
2 're not supposed to walk
3 expected me to become a doctor
4 're not meant to be
5 thirteen is supposed to be
6 meant to go back to school
7 were supposed to visit
8 people are expected to take part
3 1 can't
2 mustn't
3 had to go
4 can't have
5 don't have to
6 can't have been
7 must have been
8 must have gone out
4 1 could hardly sleep
2 could only see

3 could hardly have anticipated
4 could easily have had / could have easily had
5 should also have had
6 could barely move
7 can ever make up
8 should never have booked
5 1 *correct*
2 must already have arrived / must have arrived already
3 probably won't see
4 will never admit
5 will probably win
6 We could hardly see
7 We can also provide
8 *correct*

Unit 10

1 1 b
2 a
2 at all this traffic
3 1 *correct*
2 this money
3 these changing times
4 these children
5 *correct*
6 these days
7 this work
8 this knowledge

Unit 11

1 1 b
2 b
2 many different kinds of music
3 1 number
2 amount
3 kind
4 sorts
5 number
6 amount
7 type
8 sort

Unit 12

1 1 b
2 b
2 I see some seats in the back row

3 1 on the fourth floor
2 an automatic washing machine
3 the best results ever
4 the exact date
5 the bride's close friends
6 the arrival time
7 a few suggestions
8 a high standard

Test 4

1 1 these
2 this
3 that
4 these
5 those
6 this
7 those
8 this

2 1 a large number
2 different types
3 a large amount of office equipment
4 sorts of jobs
5 *correct*
6 other kinds of accommodation
7 kind of information
8 *correct*

3 1 for electronic gadgets
2 these days
3 all kinds of
4 *correct*
5 the electronic equipment
6 the gadget
7 a treadmill
8 *correct*

4 1 the
2 the
3 the
4 the
5 a
6 the
7 The
8 a
9 an / the
10 The
11 —
12 a
13 the

14 a
15 The
16 an

Unit 13

1 1 b
2 a

2 you for your attention

3 1 Yours
2 yours
3 you; your
4 your
5 your; you
6 you're
7 your; you
8 you

Unit 14

1 1 b
2 a

2 for giving me a second chance

3 1 chances
2 chance
3 opportunities
4 opportunity
5 possibility
6 opportunity
7 chance
8 opportunity

Unit 15

1 1 a
2 a

2 this year's event was a disappointment

3 1 event
2 activity
3 event
4 meeting
5 event
6 organisation
7 activities
8 programme

Test 5

1 1 for this opportunity
2 equal opportunities
3 a second chance
4 are opportunities for
5 opportunities are available

6 same chance
7 slim chance
8 *correct*
2 1 you're
2 your
3 your
4 you
5 yours
6 your
7 you're
8 yours
3 1 events
2 programme
3 event
4 programme
5 activities
6 meeting
7 activities
8 event
4 1 your
2 you're
3 opportunities
4 your
5 you
6 you
7 yours
8 chances
9 opportunities
10 you're
11 events
12 your
13 you
14 organisation
15 activity
16 Opportunities

Unit 16
1 1 b
2 a
2 open from 8 am to 10 pm
3 1 concerned
2 *correct*
3 true
4 open
5 sports / sporting
6 dramatic
7 variety
8 cultural

Unit 17
1 1 b
2 b
2 a small business, but we have plans to expand
3 1 great
2 large / small
3 wide / limited / narrow
4 short
5 high
6 light
7 small
8 false

Unit 18
1 1 b
2 a
2 we don't serve breakfast dishes at lunchtime
3 1 worldwide
2 air conditioning
3 hairdresser
4 lifestyle
5 *correct*
6 so-called
7 free time
8 *correct*

Test 6
1 1 of great importance
2 a large quantity
3 is limited
4 quite low
5 a great success
6 bad habits
7 *correct*
8 inaccurate information
2 1 dramatically
2 open
3 sports
4 cultural
5 concerned
6 varied
7 true
8 sport
3 1 brand-new
2 grown up
3 easy-going

4 well known
5 breathtaking
6 middle-aged
7 English-speaking
8 free time
4 1 Sport
2 well-liked
3 *correct*
4 four years
5 worldwide
6 top-class
7 well-known
8 *correct*
9 *correct*
10 cultural
11 short holiday
12 living rooms
13 *correct*
14 high wages
15 *correct*
16 great

Unit 19
1 1 b
2 a
2 advice to you is to be very tolerant
3 1 complaint
2 complain
3 life
4 paid
5 seats
6 advice
7 complaints
8 stay

Unit 20
1 1 b
2 b
2 I'm looking for something inexpensive
3 1 inadequate
2 misunderstood
3 improper
4 dissatisfaction
5 unsatisfactory
6 incomplete
7 non-native
8 unforgettable

Unit 21
1 1 b
2 a
2 I'd like to speak to you regarding a pay rise
3 1 Regarding / As for the hotel
2 Regarding / As regards the entertainment
3 Regarding / As regards the variety
4 Regarding / As regards these complaints
5 *correct*
6 my advice regarding passing
7 Regarding / As regards the new clubroom
8 *correct*

Test 7
1 1 disobedience
2 unforgettable
3 non-existent
4 disorganised
5 Unconditional
6 unconvincing
7 impractical
8 intolerable
2 1 advise
2 lives
3 regarding
4 complaints
5 stay
6 seats
7 Regarding
8 payment
3 1 *correct*
2 advice regarding improvements
3 dissatisfaction regarding the tour
4 Regarding public transport
5 points regarding the organisation
6 *correct*
7 Regarding your request
8 Regarding the danger
4 1 complaint
2 seats
3 unscheduled
4 uncomfortable
5 impolite / disorganised

6 disorganised / impolite
7 pay
8 inconvenient
5 1 non-verbal
2 independently
3 uncomfortable
4 misunderstandings
5 unconsciously
6 mislead
7 unsuccessful
8 impatience

Unit 22
1 1 b
2 b
2 I won't be able to come to your party because I'm going away that weekend
3 1 … like a refund because I'm dissatisfied …
2 … provide vegetarian food. However, there is …
3 … to accept the job. However, there are …
4 Because there was a thunderstorm, I arrived at College … / I arrived at College wet and cold because there was a thunderstorm.
5 … a beautiful cathedral. However, that was the only enjoyable …
6 … one solution to the problem. However, there are other solutions.
7 Because we think the canteen is unhygienic, we are refusing to eat there.
8 … feeling very irritable because she's tired.

Unit 23
1 1 a
2 a
2 is off school because of illness
3 1 because of
2 Because of
3 because of
4 for
5 by
6 because of

7 because
8 due to

Unit 24
1 1 b
2 a
2 and see whether or not you like her / and see if / whether you like her or not
3 1 if / whether
2 whether
3 if
4 if
5 whether
6 if / whether
7 whether
8 if / whether

Test 8
1 1 because of my dissatisfaction
2 *correct*
3 because of the pass rates
4 because it hasn't
5 by the dog
6 thank you for your invitation
7 happened for many reasons
8 *correct*
2 1 *correct*
2 The Party Conference ended successfully. However, a lot of issues were not discussed.
3 Because he was feeling unwell, he decided not to attend the meeting.
4 I used to keep fit. However, I've been too busy of late to do so.
5 *correct*
6 Due to the difficulties the firm experienced, they had to close down.
7 If you want to see the beginning of the film, you'll have to hurry.
8 *correct*
3 1 if
2 if
3 whether
4 whether
5 though
6 If

7 Although
8 if

4 1 If
2 because
3 because
4 However
5 if / whether
6 whether
7 if
8 Although
9 because
10 if
11 whether
12 if / whether
13 However
14 because of
15 If
16 If

Unit 25

1 1 a
2 b

2 put the posters up / put up the posters and I'll post the leaflets

3 1 put enthusiasm into everything
2 put in a lot of work / put a lot of work in
3 put into this event
4 put your ideas into practice
5 to put on an extra performance / put an extra performance on
6 put these pictures up / put up these pictures
7 putting on your coat / putting your coat on
8 put that in the right place

Unit 26

1 1 b
2 b

2 most of our time shopping

3 1 *correct*
2 paid for all our meals
3 *correct*
4 in Madrid
5 pay for the tickets
6 at the theatre

7 on the holiday
8 with my family

Unit 27

1 1 b
2 b

2 draw your attention to the graph, please

3 1 to
2 in
3 to
4 for
5 for
6 in
7 in
8 for

Test 9

1 1 pay your entrance fee
2 dissatisfaction with the service
3 *correct*
4 pay attention to the traffic
5 responsible for what has gone wrong
6 put into preparing
7 interested in knowing
8 income on rent

2 1 for
2 to
3 on
4 of
5 at
6 in
7 for
8 in

3 1 purpose of this message
2 you've put in
3 has ever put on
4 reviews in the local papers
5 *correct*
6 put into practice
7 your attention to the change
8 put up the posters / put the posters up

4 1 in
2 to
3 forward
4 for
5 on
6 in

7 for
8 for
9 on
10 —

5 1 paid the bill
2 should pay attention to
3 like to put forward
4 draw your attention to
5 put your ideas into practice
6 spends a lot of money on

Unit 28

1 1 a
2 b

2 for business from 8.00 to 8.00.

3 1 recommend
2 environment
3 necessary
4 committee
5 career
6 disappointing
7 colleagues
8 exaggerated

Unit 29

1 1 a
2 b

2 not licensed to serve alcohol. Cheques not accepted.

3 1 colour
2 cheque
3 centre
4 neighbour
5 *correct*
6 programmes
7 *correct*
8 humour

Unit 30

1 1 b
2 b

2 like to speak to a police officer, please

3 1 children
2 toilet / lavatory
3 money
4 virus
5 going to
6 pounds

7 police officer
8 friend

Test 10

1 1 accommodation
2 recommend
3 comfortable
4 committee
5 business
6 attractive
7 professional
8 different

2 1 metres
2 behaviour
3 practise
4 programmes
5 favourites
6 cheque
7 theatre
8 labourer

3 1 Labour
2 *correct*
3 environment
4 government
5 disappointed
6 Choices
7 opportunities
8 necessary

4 1 children
2 stupid
3 money
4 police officer
5 pounds
6 tolerate
7 fools
8 friends

5 1 neighbours
2 millennium
3 exaggerate
4 According
5 colleagues
6 negotiate
7 careers
8 rumour

Acknowledgements

I would like to thank Jenny Letham for her advice and encouragement.

Illustrated by Julian Mosedale

The publishers are grateful to the following for permission for the use of copyright material:
p44 Extract from De Bono's Thinking Course by Edward De Bono reproduced with the permission of BBC Worldwide Limited. Copyright © Edward De Bono 1982

The Cambridge Learner Corpus
This book is based on information from the Cambridge Learner Corpus, a collection of over 60,000 exam papers from Cambridge ESOL. It shows real mistakes students make, and highlights which parts of English cause particular problems for learners.

The Cambridge Learner Corpus has been developed jointly with the University of Cambridge ESOL Examinations and forms part of the Cambridge International Corpus.

To find out more, visit
www.cambridge.org/elt/corpus